BR Design

people who listen. interiors that work.

Published by:
Visual Profile Books, Inc.
389 Fifth Avenue, New York, NY 10016
Phone: 212.279.7000
www.visualprofilebooks.com

Distributed by:
National Book Networks, Inc.
15200 NBN Way, Blue Ridge Summit, PA 17214
Toll Free (U.S.): 800.462.6420
Toll Free Fax (U.S.): 800.338.4550
Email orders or Inquires: customercare@nbnbooks.com

ISBN 13: 978-1-7362731-4-2

Library of Congress Cataloging in Publication Data: BR Design: people who listen. interiors that work.
Book Designer: Christina Chin
Editor: Roger Yee

BR Design

people who listen. interiors that work.

VISUAL PROFILE BOOKS, NEW YORK

CONTENTS

INTRODUCTION

Welcome to the world of BR Design Associates, where the collaboration between exceptional design and attentive client input gives rise to breathtakingly beautiful spaces. With an unwavering belief that man-made environments should excel in both form and function, we have been at the forefront of the design industry since our establishment in 1985. As an award-winning interior design firm based in New York, we have had the privilege of serving clients across diverse fields such as finance, advertising, law, and entertainment.

What sets BR Design apart from the rest is our unwavering commitment to listening intently to our clients' desires and expectations. We view design as a cooperative endeavor, fostering a dialogue between our talented designers and our esteemed clients. This collaboration within our team ensures that each project is infused with diverse perspectives and unique insights, resulting in extraordinary spaces that reflect the distinct essence of our clients.

Founder and Principal, Michael Rait, ASID, has always had a deep passion for aesthetics and design. Starting his creative journey at a young age, Michael's artistic abilities, determination, and supportive parents led him to pursue a career in design. His time at Parsons School of Design further honed his skills and instilled in him the value of teamwork in the design process.

Michael's amibtion was to one day lead his own firm, a goal inspired by his father and other family members. Anticipating that building a successful design firm requires a unique set of skills much different than working for one, Michael assembled a dedicated team of associates when he founded BR Design. Their shared commitment to delivering the best possible outcomes for clients has been the foundation of the company's success. We understand that our clients entrust us with their time and resources, and we prioritize their culture and aspirations above all else, crafting spaces that truly enhance their lifestyles and work environments.

"My firm survived and prospered by doing the best possible job for our clients," Michael states. "Designers always say they will do this. We really meant it, remembering that we were using our clients' time and money to support their cultures, not indulge in monuments to ourselves."

Our collaborative culture extends beyond our client relationships, fostering mentorship opportunities between senior and junior designers within our firm. This commitment to cultivating homegrown talent ensures that BR Design thrives not only in the present but also secures a promising future.

As in any business, design firms are impacted by the country's economic cycles, rising and falling, as the economy and real estate markets fluctuate. Throughout the firm's history, BR Design has been able to weather these cycles through strong relationships with loyal clients and referrals from a broad business and personal network, which look to BR Design as a valued partner and resource.

OUR MISSION

At BR Design, attentive listening forms the core of our approach. We believe that by genuinely hearing our clients, we gain invaluable insights into their deepest aspirations. This understanding serves as the bedrock upon which we build substantial designs infused with creativity, meticulous attention to detail, and exceptional customer service.

Our team possesses a wealth of creativity, profound product knowledge, construction expertise, and unwavering professionalism. These qualities enable us to seamlessly execute our clients' project goals, breathing life into their visions. We recognize that each project holds its own unique nature, and we emphasize the significance of continuous communication throughout the design process. By maintaining open lines of dialogue, we ensure that costly delays or the need for redesign are minimized, fostering a smooth and efficient journey from conception to realization.

Listening to what our clients need. Applying specialized team experience to the unique problems of specific business categories.

Translating what we hear into a design that supports a client's efficiency by enhancing their image and bringing their vision to life.

Communicating every step of the way, we can make the process smoother and eliminate surprises and stress.

Delivering interiors that work.

You're invited to explore the multifaceted world of BR Design. Witness our unwavering dedication to listening, our meticulous design process, and our commitment to delivering interiors that not only inspire but also function flawlessly. Each page showcases our passion, creativity, and attention to detail, offering you a glimpse into the transformative power of exceptional design.

IN THE STUDIO

Since 1985, BR Design has remained faithful to a single core belief: there is nothing more important in the design process than listening carefully to our clients. We firmly believe that attentive listening, from the very first interaction to the final stages, is the fundamental factor that sets our firm apart. On the foundation of this "open ears" policy, we balance the highest standards of design and client services resulting in facilities planning and corporate interior design that consistently work – design that delivers both aesthetic impact and enhanced operational efficiencies. BR Design has developed a client base – Fortune 500 companies, Not-for-Profit organizations, and privately owned businesses – and has designed facilities from national headquarters to high-tech installations. Currently, we have more than a dozen real estate owners as clients. 75% of our corporate design projects are based upon repeat business from our satisfied clients.

At BR Design, sustainability and socially responsible building practices are paramount. As proud members of the US Green Building Council, we firmly believe in the long-term impact of sustainable design on our environment. By integrating sustainable principles into our work, we create spaces that not only captivate visually but also contribute positively to our planet.

"Architecture should speak of its time and place, but yearn for timelessness."

- Frank Ghery

THE DESIGN PROCESS

The design process at BR Design unfolds through several carefully orchestrated phases, with our dedicated team members guiding every step of the way. We commence with the programming phase, where we delve into understanding space requirements and meticulously gather information on the site and our client's specific needs. Next, we undertake space studies and test fits to visualize the architectural potential of the area. Concurrently, we develop a comprehensive plan encompassing the project's scope of work and budget, subject to review and approval by our client.

Following the programming phase, we seamlessly transition into the schematic design phase. Here, our team at BR Design meticulously crafts alternative space studies and layouts, ensuring that all requirements, practical considerations, and aesthetic preferences are met. We then present a comprehensive design showcase to our clients, encompassing various elements of the project, ranging from furniture and lighting to doors and wall finishes. Through detailed renderings, we provide our clients with a vivid visual representation of how their space will come together harmoniously.

Once budgets, planning, and presentations receive the client's approval, BR Design proceeds to prepare architectural construc-

tion documents. These documents serve as essential blueprints for contractors to bid on. After thorough analysis, the contract for construction is awarded to a trusted general contractor who remains in constant contact with our team. To maintain seamless progress, we arrange weekly meetings involving all relevant parties, ensuring that the project stays firmly on track.

Upon the completion of construction, the final designs and carefully selected furniture are expertly implemented. Throughout the entire design process, our team maintains close collaboration with the client, diligently working to ensure that the design aligns with their needs, expectations, and vision. We remain committed to constructing spaces that not only meet our client's desires but are also built with utmost safety, efficiency, and adherence to budgetary considerations.

"Each project has its own unique identity, so it's fun to collaborate with each client to merge their practical needs and wish-list items with our planning of their space and overall aesthetic design."

-Chase Kaars, Project Manager

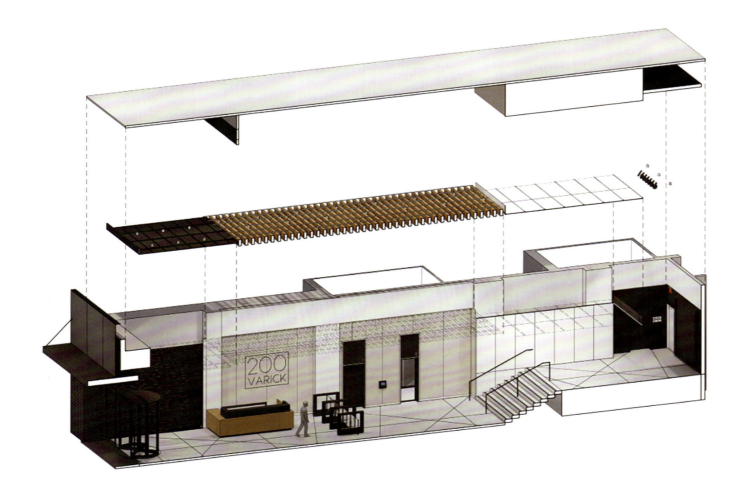

The process of interior architecture unfolds as a meticulously curated series of steps aimed at crafting interior spaces that seamlessly combine functionality and aesthetic appeal, all the while aligning with the unique needs and goals of our valued clients.

Interior architecture is the process of designing and creating functional and aesthetically pleasing interior spaces. BR Design leads our cilents through all of the phases needed to create a successful project.

1. **Programming:** The first step in the process of interior architecture is programming. This involves gathering information about the client's needs, goals, and requirements for the space.

2. **Schematic Design:** This involves creating a design concept that reflects the client's needs and goals. The design concept includes floor plans, elevations, and 3D renderings that show the layout and design of the space.

3. **Design Development:** We refine the design and select materials, finishes, and furnishings that will be used in the space. The design development phase also includes creating detailed drawings and specifications that will be used during construction.

4. **Construction Documentation:** We will coordinate with the consultants and create detailed drawings and specifications that will be used by contractors and builders during construction. The construction documentation includes floor plans, elevations, sections, details, and schedules.

5. **Construction Administration:** BR Design will oversee the construction process to ensure that the design is being implemented correctly.

6. **Post-Occupancy Evaluation:** BR Design will conduct a post-occupancy evaluation in addition to our constant monitoring. This involves gathering feedback from the client and occupants of the space to identify areas for improvement and to ensure that the design meets the client's needs and goals.

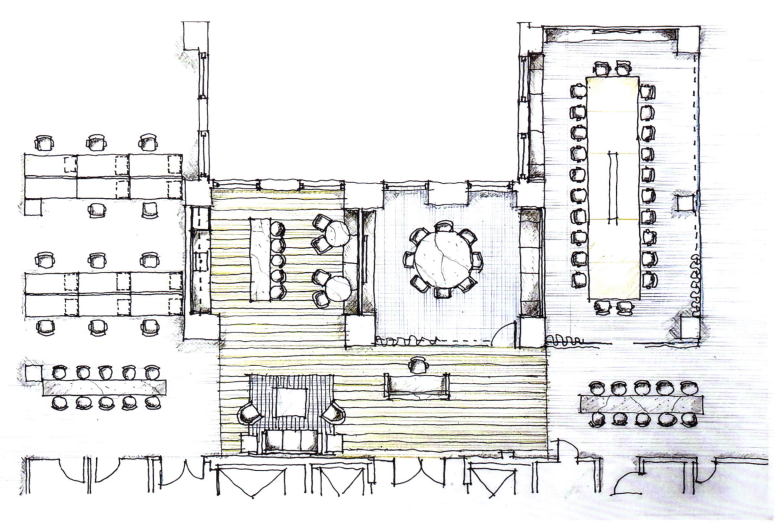

Reverence Capital

New York, New York

Reverence Capital is a private investment firm, founded in 2013, focusing on thematic investing in leading global, middle-market financial services and opportunistic, structured credit and credit-related investments. The firm's new, one-floor, 15,000-square-foot office in midtown Manhattan is a crisply detailed, elegantly furnished and subtly illuminated contemporary space. While reduced to its essentials, the 50-person facility comes alive with the architectural geometries of its triangular floor plan, the effective use of furnishings to define space, and the role that façades of neighboring office towers play in providing color and pattern. The reception area, private and shared offices, conference rooms, 25-person boardroom, and other shared areas are arranged around the central core, with glass-fronted perimeter offices bringing the panoramic view of the city indoors. The boardroom is a main feature, incorporating distinctive lighting, marble and lacquered millwork, multi-media wall, and display wall for artwork. Modern design and technology converge here in a uniquely New York moment.

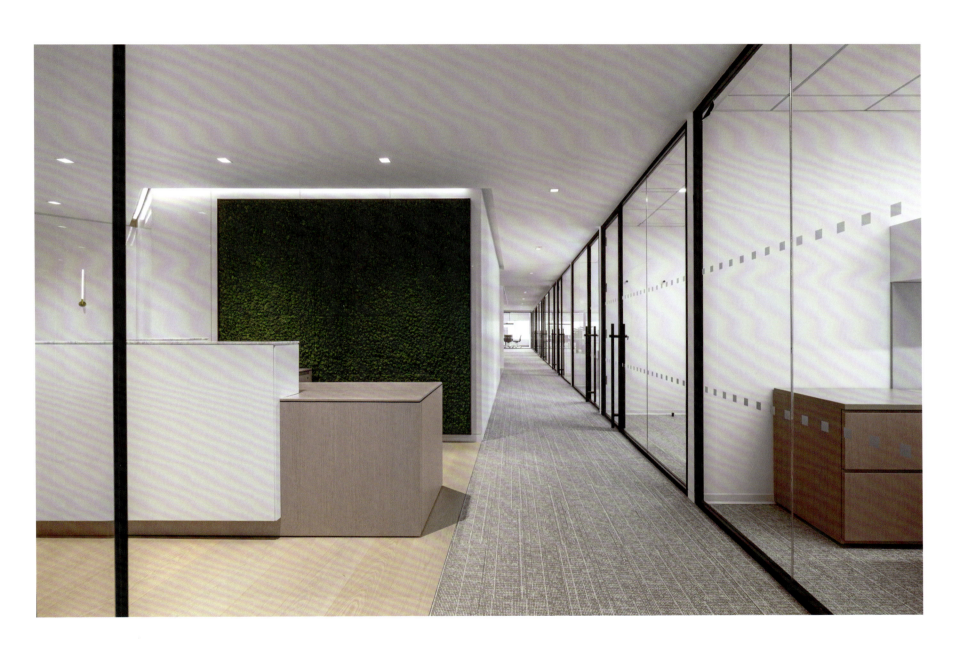

Mane

New York, USA

Consumers may never know that the essence of many of the foods and fragrances they enjoy originate in the enterprise of Victor Mane, who founded a distillery in 1871 in south France to produce fragrant materials from regional flowers and plants. Today, businesses in 39 countries depend on products from the Mane Group, backed by 27 manufacturing plants, 50 R&D centers and 77 offices worldwide, led by Jean Mane, a member of the fifth generation of the founding family. BR Design's design of a two-floor, 15,562-square-foot New York space for Mane USA reflects the importance of the site, comprising a sales office, innovation center and fine fragrance studio. The facility has been conceived with an open plan where perfumers and evaluators at unassigned workstations and enclosed spaces provide high-performance air circulation so odors can be properly extracted for perfumers to smell. Organized by teams for sales and marketing, logistics, perfumer and evaluator, and management with ample collaborative areas, the design uses natural materials (stressing organic and green sources), glass and copper and black metal detailing to create a modern, minimal environment that is both functional and chic. A mixture of pendant and cove lighting provide sophisticated finishing touches.

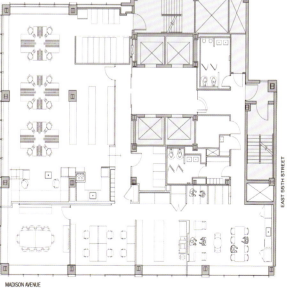

Daily Pay

New York, New York

DailyPay's workforce in Manhattan's Financial District occupies a spacious, airy and inviting modern office on two floors totaling 130,000-square-feet, their new office space is comprised of private offices, open work areas, conference rooms and a variety of amenities, including lounges, pantries and game rooms, resulting in a stylish and distinctive setting for some 600 employees. By listening very carefully to their clients, BR Design responded by taking into consideration such key management issues as job functions, privacy, and departmental organization. The design team strove to exploit the existing architecture as much as possible, thereby reducing costs and minimizing disruption, while introducing new elements specific to the daily activities and corporate culture of DailyPay, that would give the facility a more personalized and effective space. The designer's unique use of standard construction materials and modern furnishings has given the firm an efficient space that reinforces their brand and has helped them attract and retain their talented staff.

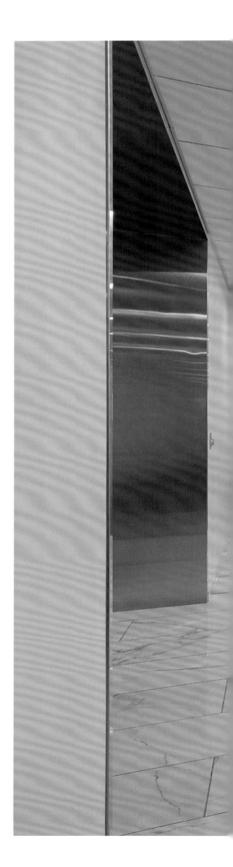

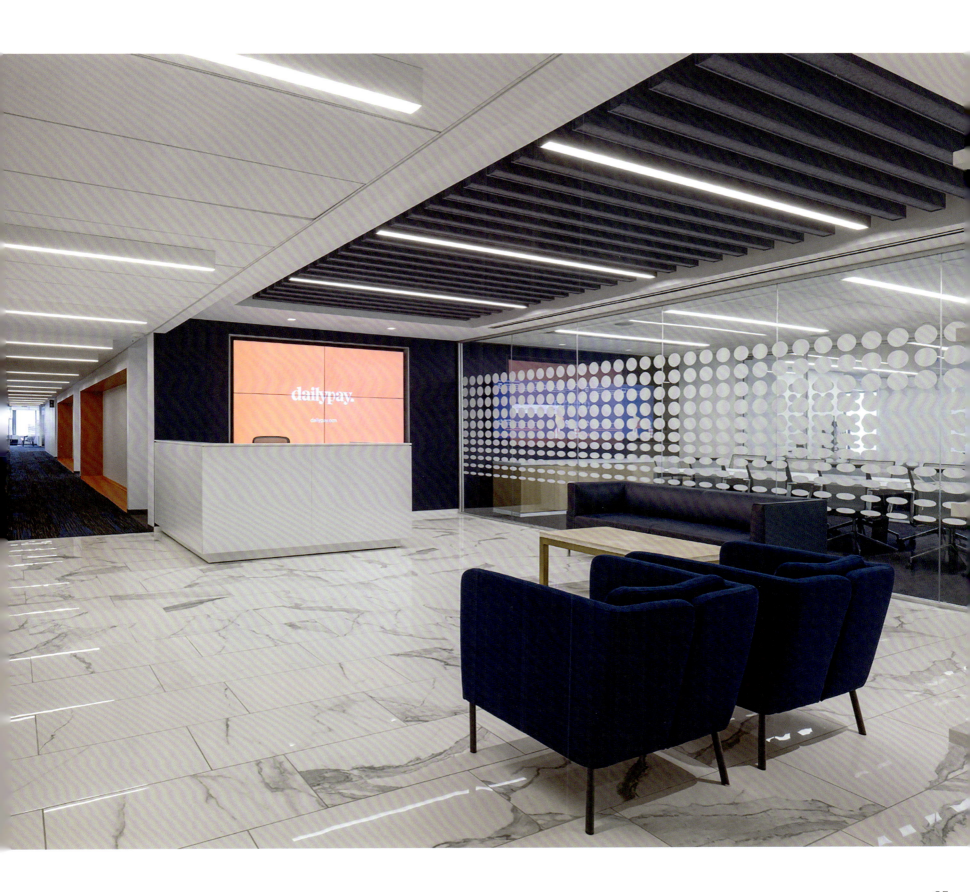

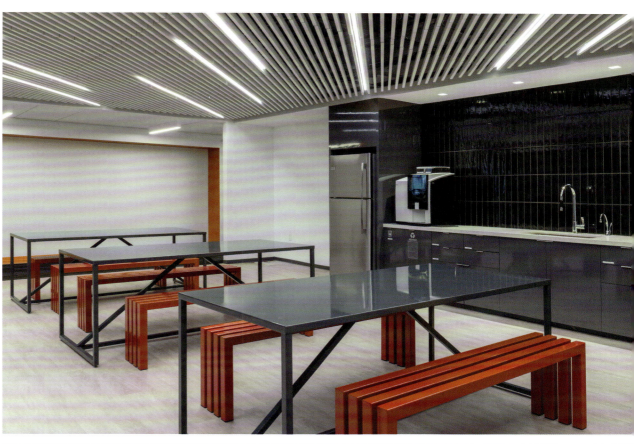

Marx Realty

New York, New York

Since 2020, the historic pandemic has caused many commercial office tenants to question the need for offices, forcing landlords and developers to respond to remain competitive. Marx Realty recently made major investments in two midtown Manhattan buildings, introducing new and renovated façades, lobbies, and amenities. 10 Grand Central is a 36-story, 400,000-square-foot Art Deco structure dating from 1931, designed by Ely Jacques Kahn. To promote leasing, BR Design designed pre-built office suites at 10 Grand Central. BR Design's interiors feature glass fronted private offices, open work and collaborative areas, conference rooms, and reception areas with beautiful cafés. The designs incorporates visual cues from its surroundings. Elements such as exposed ceilings and ductwork attractively rearranging overhead to maximize existing ceiling heights. The results exceded expectations and the space at 10 Grand Central has been cited by Crain's as one of the best places to work in New York.

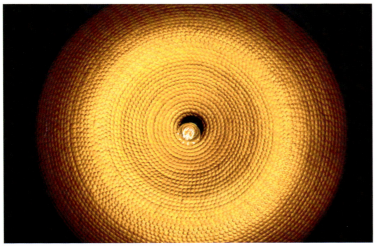

Brunello Cucinelli

New York, New York

High-end clothing, footwear and accessories by Italian fashion designer Brunello Cucinelli are prized for their contemporary style, luxurious materials and meticulous craftsmanship. Visitors to the new, 12,000-square-foot, New York showroom will be pleased to immerse themselves in an environment that embraces the brand's design philosophy. The showroom has a modern hospitality vibe, with large individual client zones equipped for various simulations gatherings within a continuous spatial environment. This functionality is successful due to the skillful placement of archtectural elements, such as a fireplace as one focal point, luminous display millwork, and jewel-like metal and glass partitions which establish porous boundaries. Every detail counts, from unique wood veneers, flawless Italian millwork, and fine hardwood flooring to precision metal and glass components, sleek modern furnishings and sophisticated lighting. This commitment to high quality should not surprise the fashion industry. Cucilnelli describes his enterprise as an embodiment of "humanistic capitalism" and "human sustainability." Based in Solomeo, the designer devotes time and personal resources to restoring historic village. His New York showroom reflects his passion for great design, commitment to quality and his attention to detail perfectly.

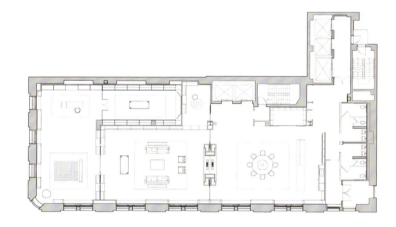

Project Renewal

New York, New York

Project Renewal is a non-profit organization founded in 1967 to help eradicate homelessness through retraining, employment and affordable housing developments. Through programs that provide health services, emergency, transitional, and permanent housing, and employment services to connect clients with meaningful jobs, Project Renewal helps some 16,000 individuals yearly. BR Design provided the full scope of planning and design services for the organization's new, one-floor, 40,000-square-foot corporate office located within a vintage printing press building in New York's Tribeca neighborhood. Conceived to accommodate growth and improve efficiency, the contemporary workspace features open-plan work areas along the perimeter exterior window walls and glass-fronted interior offices, accommodating training and counseling areas, administrative offices, meeting rooms and interview areas. The spacious proportions and robust architecture of the base building inspired the design team to effectively incorporate such existing construction details as exposed high ceilings slabs, exposed round columns with flaring capitals, and industrial windows into the clean, informal and functional interiors, which are appointed in attractive, modern furnishings. Triangular-shaped LED lighting fixtures echoing Project Renewal's logo and color scheme give the facility a look that reinforces the organization's identity.

The Greer Cabaret Theatre

Pittsburgh, Pennsylvania

Performing arts venues are among today's secular temples, and the Greer Cabaret Theater, located within the Michael Graves-designed Theater Square Garage in Pittsburgh's Cultural District, is a cultural icon cherished by local theatergoers. Before the Greer embarked on its second decade, its operator, the Pittsburgh Cultural Trust, held a competition to transform its black box format into an intimate cabaret venue on a par with such New York venues as Joe's Pub and 54 Below. In addition, the Trust sought to reconfigure its beloved Backstage Bar, dropping from 250 seats to 200 to support small-scaled musical acts while enhancing its popular food and beverage service, to integrate the lobbies for the box office and bar as a single, grand space, and to give the Greer visibility on the street, producing what Scott Shiller, senior vice president of the Trust, described as a "street to seat experience." The renovation proposed by BR Design ushered patrons into a sleek, spacious lobby opening simultaneously to the theater and the bar, imparting a crisp, contemporary look to the cabaret beneath an orbital chandelier, and turning the bar into an illuminated, jewel-like object to make evenings at the Greer sparkle in more ways than one.

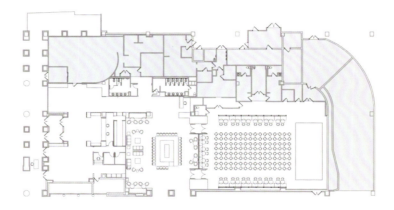

Resorts World New York

Queens, New York

Proudly proclaiming itself the only casino in New York City, Resorts World New York City opened in October 2011 in Jamaica, Queens, and quickly became the leading slot machine revenue generator in the United States, bringing in nearly $700 million in revenue and 10 million visitors in 2012. BR Design was recently retained to update existing facilities, a critical strategy that keeps casino environments fresh for established clientele and attractive to newcomers. For Resort World's Liberty Bar and Atrium, the designers made these spaces feel new and modern while blending with the casino's overall ambience. BR Design's scheme combined lively contemporary design and trendy materials such as laser-cut metal, backlit wall panels, and jewel toned finishes with luxurious furnishings, bold colors, and glamorous theatrical lighting to introduce new energy and excitement. Among the immediate results is the way the Liberty Bar, newly transformed by a gracefully flowing and more open layout, now successfully draws guests to pause briefly for drinks before returning to the games. Creative design has repeatedly shown its ability to enhance the gaming experience, and BR Design has dealt Resorts World a winning hand.

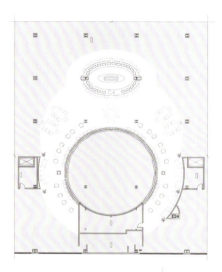

U.S. Citizenship and Immigration Services

Brooklyn, New York

As an agency of the U.S. Department of Homeland Security that administers the nation's naturalization and immigration system, the U.S. Citizenship and Immigration Services (USCIS) is where such immigration matters as applications for work visas, asylum and citizenship are processed and adjudicated. Commissioned by the General Services Administration to design a four-floor, 54,000-square-foot USCIS field office within a new, 43-story, mixed-use, high-rise project in downtown Brooklyn, BR Design is creating an environment that makes the public experience clear, functional and aesthetically pleasing. The facility's waiting rooms, interview rooms, gallery visiting area, ceremony room and connecting stair are all carefully integrated in an environment of light, openness, color and texture to bring unity, continuity and harmony to a multi-floor setting in the podium of the building. Materials and finishes include such attractive details as wood batten ceilings, terrazzo floors, wood veneer millwork, and innovative architectural lighting, complemented by a color palette of warm neutrals accented by the use of bold color. Whatever purpose brings the public to the new Brooklyn field office, USCIS will express a warm welcome to all.

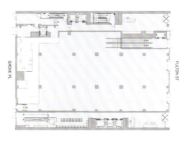

Marx Realty

New York, New York

To enter Kohlberg & Company's midtown Manhattan office is to encounter a distinctive and uncommonly handsome workplace—a modern, moody and masculine environment that speaks of expertise, integrity, strength and vision. It is an apt image. The 7,414-square-foot facility has been expressly designed by BR Design to give 25-30 employees of this private equity firm, founded in 1987 by Jerome Kohlberg, Jr., a co-founder of the prominent global investment company Kohlberg Kravis Roberts, a supportive environment for investing in such transactions as leveraged buyouts, privatization procedures and acquisitions of privately held businesses. With effectiveness and collegiality in mind, the firm's workstations, private offices, conference/meeting rooms, collaborative spaces and café are configured as an open plan workplace. High quality materials, finishes and furnishings are subtly combined to create the desired ambience, incorporating natural woods, brass accents, solid surface waterfall countertops, accent tiles, fine fabrics, leathers and wallcoverings, elegant architectural lighting fixtures, and stylish contemporary furniture. There is design ingenuity as well, because ductwork, sprinklers and other overhead MEP components have been left exposed to emphasize ceiling height. Thanks to the skillful use of color and form, the ceiling suavely reinforces the office's polished look with finesse even the client can admire.

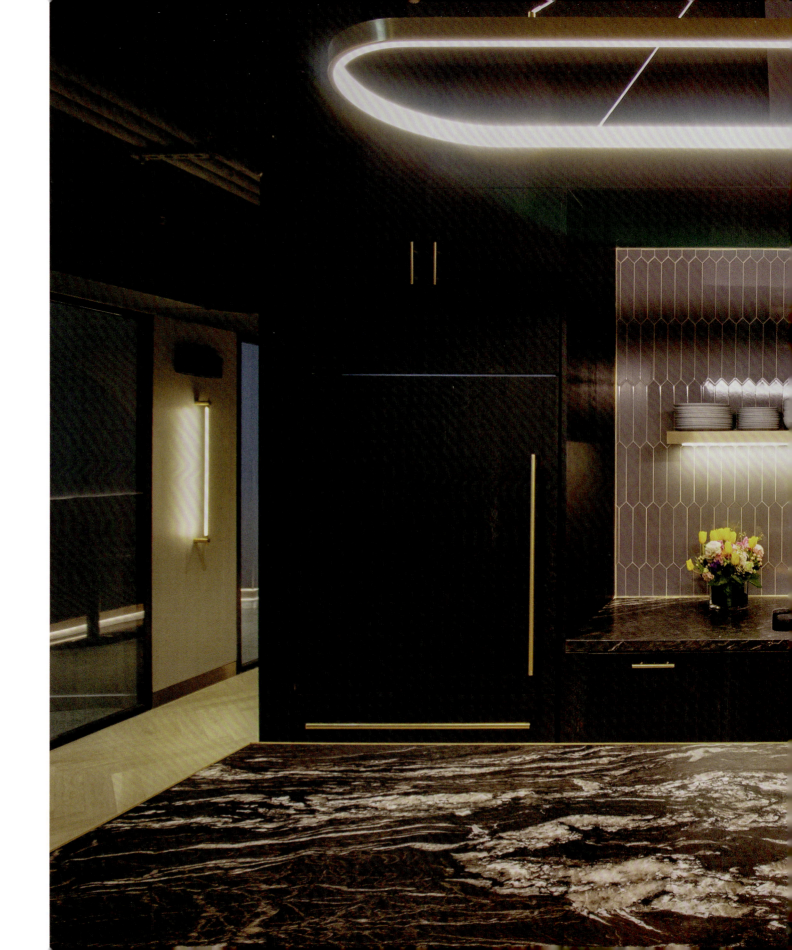

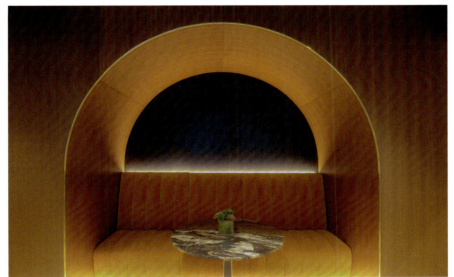

Marx Realty

New York, New York

Emerging from a major renovation, 545 Madison Avenue, a 17-story, 153,583-square-foot, International Style tower built in 1955 at the intersection of Madison Avenue and East 55th Street in midtown Manhattan, is now a Class A office building with the look, feel and personality of a luxury boutique hotel. A project of Marx Realty, a leading investor, developer and manager of commercial real estate, 545 Madison Avenue gives tenants a sumptuous work environment with state-of-the-art services in the heart of the Plaza District, a prestigious neighborhood graced by exclusive shopping, gourmet restaurants, iconic hotels, and such landmarks as Rockefeller Center, St. Patrick's Cathedral, the Chrysler Building and the Museum of Modern Art. To display the potential of the building to prospective tenants, BR Design was commissioned to design a pre-built, 6,300-square-foot office on the second floor. This bold, responsive and flexible contemporary space, featuring an elevator lobby that leads directly to a café/lounge along with private offices, open plan workstations, conference rooms, print/copy area and restrooms, is appointed in such fine materials and finishes as walnut veneer, deep-pile carpet, wood herringbone flooring, textured glass, porcelain tile and architectural lighting fixtures. The interiors constitute a lively demonstration of the power of design.

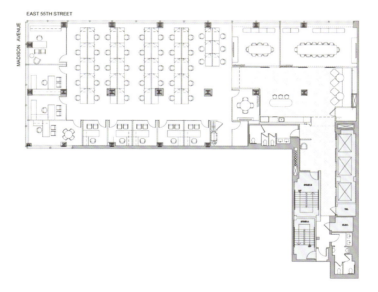

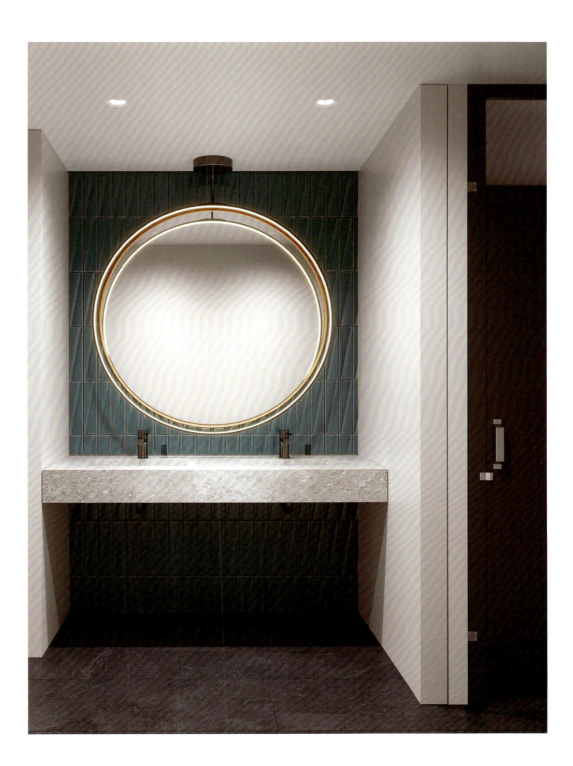

Galvanize

New York, New York

The digital economy's rapid evolution is demanding new forms of knowledge and skill, making such organizations as Galvanize, Inc. vital as educational resources. Founded in 2012, Denver-based Galvanize operates a network of urban campuses. Here, students, entrepreneurs and established companies can access needed skills, workspace and networks to reach their goals in Web development, data science and data engineering. Its New York campus designed by BR Design Associates is a two-floor, 50,000-square-foot facility scheduled for completion in 2017. A former candy factory is converted into a lively environment where the two principal areas, dedicated to schooling and co-working, form one unified space. Like other technology-oriented offices, Galvanize prizes flexibility, utilizing mobile, folding wall, community spaces, open work areas and scattered collab areas to provide a variety of environments; this space is anything but generic. Besides an LED-illuminated "tunnel" the designers created to connect the two main areas, there are such gestures to New York City as a staircase inspired by cast iron sidewalks, learning booths made of colored glass replicating subway logos, and a hidden original vaulted ceiling now left exposed. The former loading dock was converted into the campus's entrance as a coffee shop, to proudly celebrate the Big Apple's role in the digital economy.

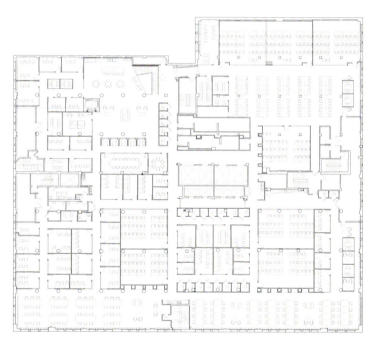

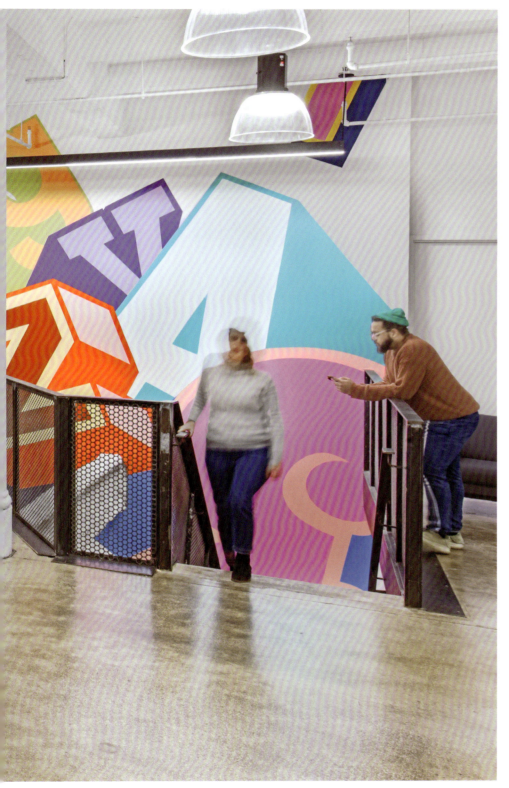

Tai Ping

New York, New York

Having designed the previous New York City showroom and offices of Tai Ping, a Hong Kong-based global custom carpet company serving the architecture and interior design community, BR Design was excited to help the company relocate to a new, 10,000 square-foot showroom. Tai Ping has come a long way since its founding in 1956, selling their commercial business in 2017 to focus on custom-made artisan products for homes, yachts and private jets, as well as doing high-end commercial installations for boutique stores, hotels, and corporate offices. BR Design began the project by updating the building program and analyzing multiple properties prior to settling on space in the Flatiron District. The new showroom and offices were installed in an elegant white interior with rich, dark accented finished, exposed ceiling, ebonized wood floor and custom rug displays that could easily be lowered from the ceiling. Here Tai Ping's carpets and rugs sparkled like jewels, and the sample room functioned as the core of the facility, a transitional zone from the showroom to the design studio that made the Tai Ping story complete and unabashedly glamourous.

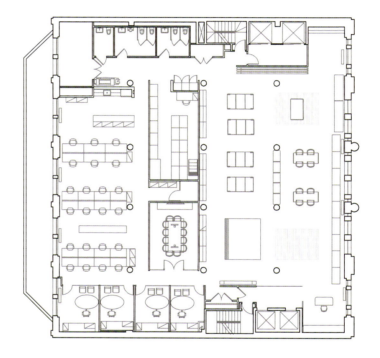

Global Citizen

New York, New York

One of the more encouraging signs that idealism is alive and well in the 21st century" vs "not dead in the 21st century is the work of Global Citizen. This international education and advocacy organization, founded in Melbourne, Australia in 2008, supports a worldwide movement to end extreme poverty, promote social justice, and combat climate change. Working in collaboration with a wide range of prominent individuals, businesses and institutions, the non-profit "action platform" has been involved in creating multimedia presentations, fellowships, fundraising campaigns, festivals and other activities that advance its goals, raising some $48.4 billion in pledges to Global Citizen-supported causes as of July 2020. In the years since its founding, it has opened offices in London, Berlin, Toronto, Lagos and Johannesburg, and relocated its headquarters in New York. To give Global Citizen a fitting headquarters in Manhattan's trendy NoHo neighborhood, BR Design has conceived a lively and informal environment of private offices, open workstations and gathering spaces that would seem appropriate for a high-tech start-up. The contemporary interiors combine stark white walls, bold graphics, exposed ceilings, wood flooring and attractive, modern furnishings—plus a high-tech conference room that is well equipped for multi-media presentations—to perform like a steaming mug of black coffee on a Monday morning.

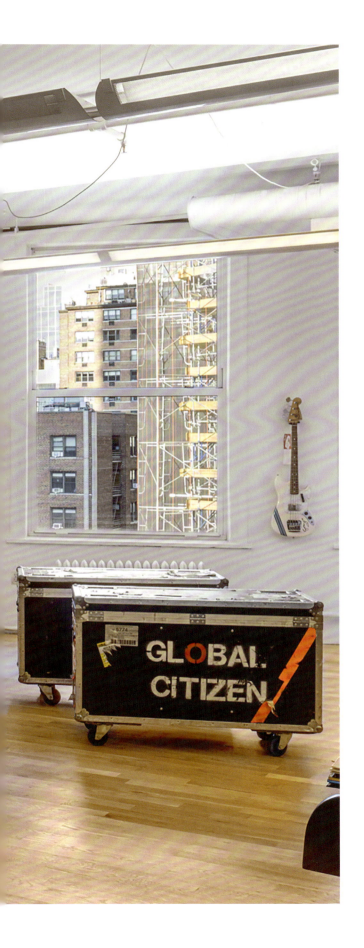

200 Varick Street Lobby

New York, New York

A 12-story, 490,000-square-foot office building in lower Manhattan's Hudson Square district, designed by architect Frank S. Parker and completed in 1927 to serve the printing industry, is entering a new era of high-tech and multi-media businesses would have seemed highly improbable just a few years ago. However, 200 Varick Street, spanning Houston and King Streets just west of trendy SoHo, is now part of a neighborhood transformation. BR Design's goal in creating a new ground-floor lobby for 200 Varick Street was to connect the building's historic ties to the printing and graphic arts industries, as desired by the landlord, with the new generation of businesses. Its solution is a chic, luxurious and unmistakably modern environment combining the imagery of black metal hardware (like the massive printing presses that once filled the building), and walls of black and white marble and exposed brick (like printer's ink on the printed page), with a terrazzo floor, wood trellis ceiling and dramatic lighting (expressing stylish modernity). The outcome is a fresh environment that tenants and visitors find reassuringly solid yet irresistibly dynamic.

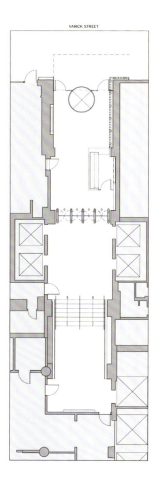

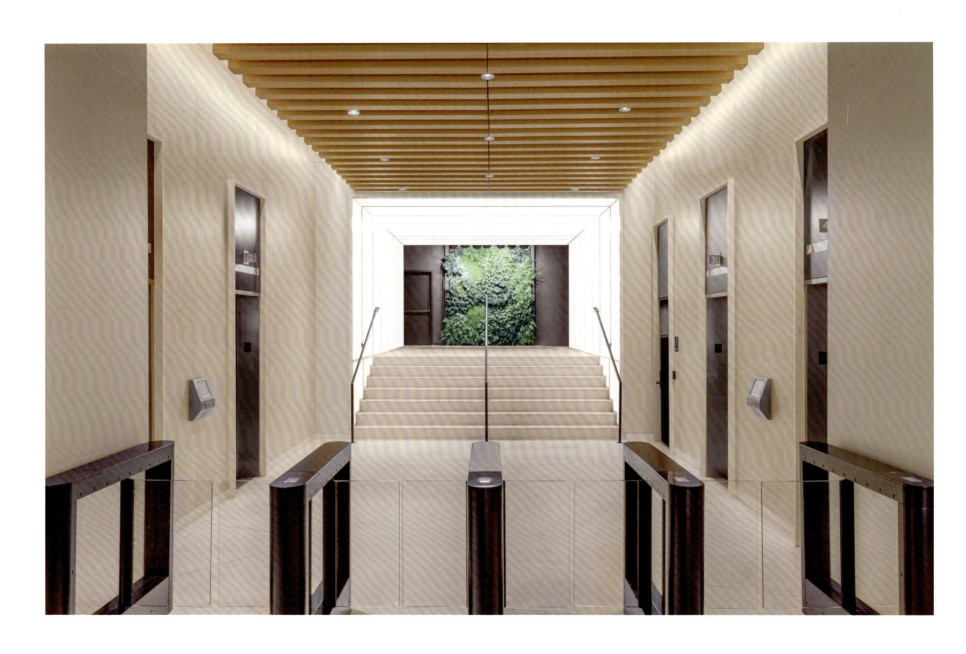

Dean & Deluca

New York, New York

In September 1977, Joel Dean, a publishing business manager, Giorgio DeLuca, a school teacher turned cheese merchant, and Jack Ceglic, an artist, opened Dean & DeLuca at 121 Prince Street in New York City's SoHo district; introducing a stylish emporium of choice gourmet foods and cookware to the creative tribe of artists, craftsmen and other bohemians dwelling in the neighborhood's industrial buildings. Dean & DeLuca became an international chain of upscale grocery stores, headquartered in Wichita, Kansas and owned since 2014 by Pace Development, a Thai real estate company. Its commission of BR Design to design a one-floor, 10,000-square-foot Manhattan corporate office for 30 employees resulted in a distinctive, contemporary workplace of private offices, open plan staff areas, conference rooms and a demonstration kitchen, bearing an unmistakable resemblance to the store's iconic, industrial-chic image. Skillfully combining white walls, white subway tile, blackened steel, polished concrete floor and warm walnut with glass office fronts framed in black satin mullions, BR Design evoked the loft-like, minimalist feel of the original Soho store. Eschewing the cramped, anonymous quarters of typical retail offices, Dean & DeLuca gave its executives and creative staff an environment as inspiring as the store itself.

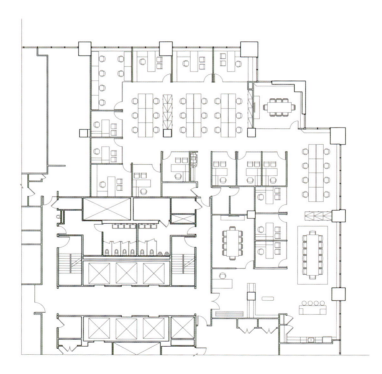

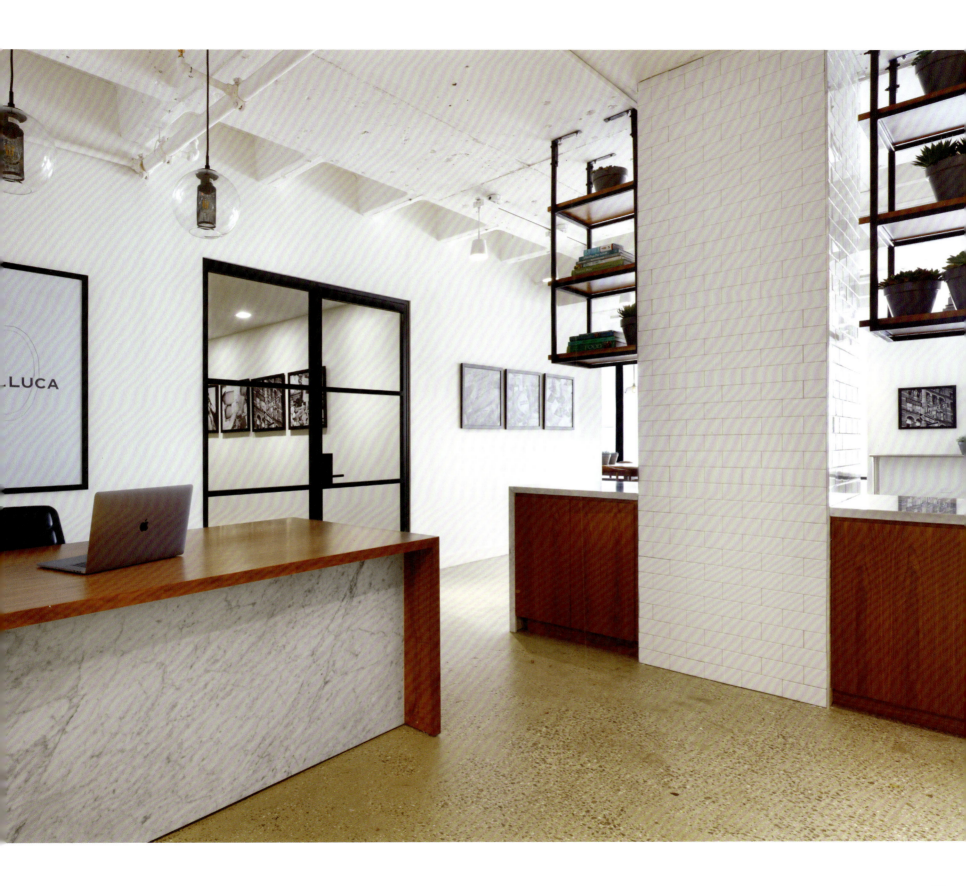

The Rohaytn Group

New York, New York

A leading specialized asset management firm that invests exclusively in emerging markets, The Rohatyn Group (TRG) was founded in 2002 by Nicolas Rohatyn, and has grown to serve clients in cities around the world, including New York where it maintains its headquarters. The form and function of TRG's one-floor, 16,000-square-foot New York office by BR Design were driven by the need to accommodate full trading capabilities and operations desks providing 24-hour market coverage as well as a staff with expertise in such areas as investment, legal and compliance, global operations and custody, risk management, marketing, investor relations and information technology. In addition, the workplace would reflect the four core traits that anchor the firm's culture, namely collegial and respectful, emphasis on teamwork, international and transparent. Complex as the design brief was, the resulting open-plan environment of workstations, glass-fronted private offices and conference rooms, open pantry and support areas gave employees and visitors a vision of clarity, logic and action that succinctly captured the unique essence of TRG.

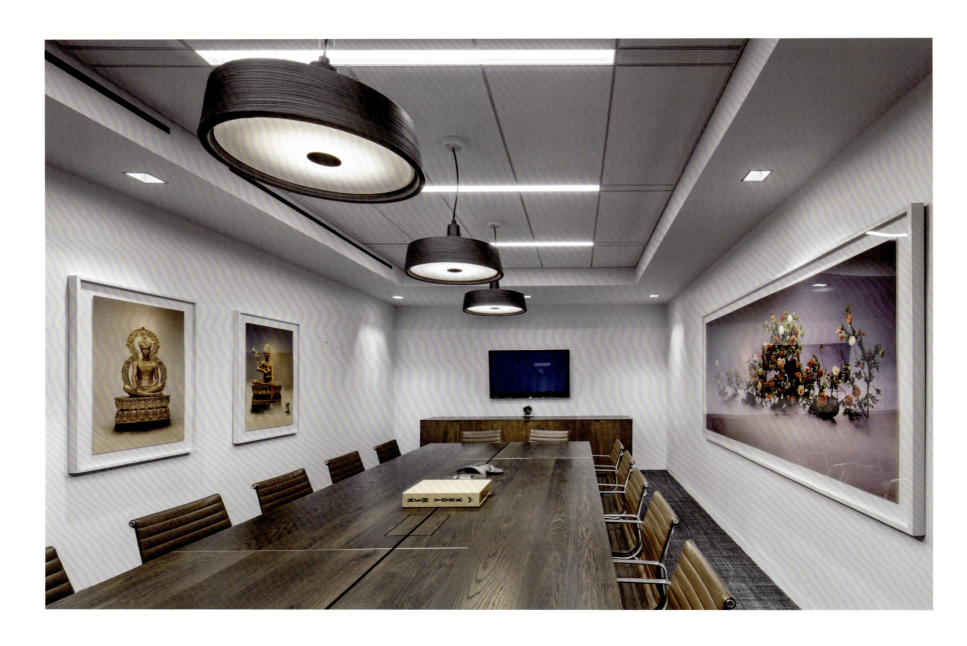

Committee to Protect Journalists

New York, New York

An independent, non-profit, non-governmental organization based in New York, the Committee to Protect Journalists (CPJ) was founded in 1981 to promote press freedom and defend the rights of journalists. Called "Journalism's Red Cross" by the American Journalism Review, CPJ works to protect and enhance free press rights within the United States, publishes a yearly international survey of press freedom called "Attacks on the Press," and compiles an annual list of all journalists killed in the line of duty around the world. The organization is a founding member of the International Freedom of Expression Exchange (IFEX), a global network of over 70 non-governmental organizations that monitors violations of free expression and defends journalists, writers, and others persecuted for exercising their right to freedom of expression. For its new office in Manhattan adjacent to Hudson Yards, BR Design created a contemporary workplace in which private offices and a conference room are housed in a glass-enclosed interior core surrounded by open work areas along the perimeter. The design is minimalistic yet entirely functional, featuring modern furnishings, carpeted floor, and glass and white drywall partitions. Its black-painted, exposed ceiling hides all the plumbing from the residences above and maximizes the building's lofty, 16-foot slab-to-slab height.

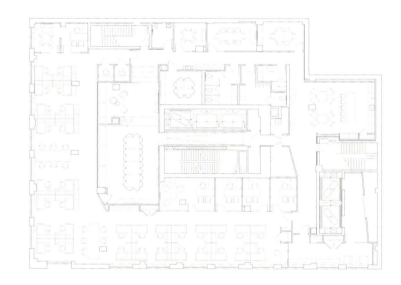

Amit Children

New York, New York

Since 1925, AMIT, an Israeli non-profit educational program, has exerted a transformative impact on Israeli education extending far beyond its schools and students. AMIT currently educates over 36,000 children in 107 schools, youth villages, surrogate family residences and other programs in 33 Israeli cities, representing Israel's only government-recognized network of religious Jewish education incorporating academic and technological studies. Critically, because two-thirds of AMIT students come from socio-economically disadvantaged communities or development towns, AMIT enables them to aspire to a better future by significantly narrowing the gaps between them and those in more affluent cities and towns in central Israel. Thus, the bulk of donor funds help level the playing field for AMIT students by providing the highest quality interactive education, additional tutoring hours, emotional support and encouragement, and cutting-edge teaching techniques. The new, 11,000-square foot, one-floor New York office for AMIT Children, designed by BR Design, acts as a liaison between AMIT and supporters in the United States. Located in Manhattan's Garment District, the facility consists of a central core of glass-enclosed conference rooms and offices flanked by open workstations lining the periphery. This arrangement maximizes the amount of daylight entering the office and enables everyone to share outdoor views.

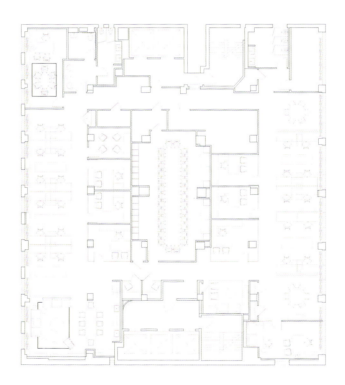

Noodle Factory

Long Island City, New York

Vibrant cities reinvent themselves, and New York is no exception. Long Island City, a residential and commercial neighborhood in the borough of Queens, has transformed itself repeatedly to meet changing circumstances. Incorporated as an independent city in1870, it became part of greater New York in 1898, thriving as a home to countless factories. With their original operations largely shuttered by the 1970s, many of these robust structures have found new lives. The former Silvercup bakery, for example, became Silvercup Studios in 1983, producing such memorable television programs as 30 Rock, Sex and the City and The Sopranos. The Noodle Factory, built in 1913 to manufacture noodles, is a six-story, 118,500-square-foot, mixed-use hybrid office facility that has benefitted from renovations and upgrades to its lobby, corridors, elevators, windows and restrooms. For its new 1,500-square-foot lobby, the owner engaged BR Design to create a space to complement such potential uses as showrooms, research and development, light manufacturing, education and corporate offices while complying with ADA requirements. The lobby now projects a stylish, high-tech look—a composition of white and wood-paneled walls, futuristic lighting, terrazzo floors, and metal and wood stair and railings—that is as fresh as the new century it serves.

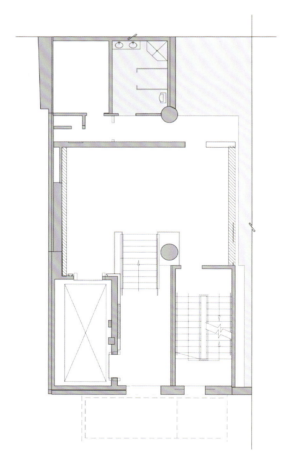

Assouline

New York, New York

Paris-based, luxury book publishing house-and lifestyle designer Assouline was founded by Prosper and Martine Assouline in 1994 and suavely courts the professional and social worlds of architecture, art, design, fashion, gastronomy, lifestyle, photography and travel documentaries. They do this by linking its books and prints, home furnishings, gifts and accessories to sophisticated marketing, promotional and cultural events. The company commissioned BR Design to design its 10,000-square-foot New York office. It requested a work environment as clean, open and stylish as the art galleries, fashion salons, retail boutiques and four-star restaurants its readers frequent. Spare and handsome as the final result was, achieving the right look for a space comprising reception, open office, private offices, executive offices, conference room, studio, pantry and restrooms required close attention to detail. The exposed waffle slab became a major element in the design of the open area, creating a strong pattern in the ceiling. In addition, a furniture plan was devised to incorporate furniture, art and antiquities that Assouline would relocate. Open and enclosed offices were carefully aligned to balance skyline views with book displays and bookshelves. A color scheme featuring Assouline's signature taupe provided the finishing touch to this one-of-a-kind environment.

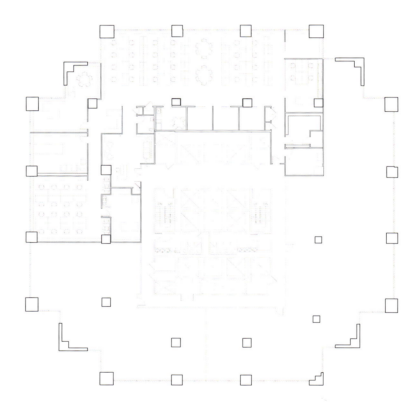

Maison Assouline

Dubai, United Arab Emirates

BR Design immediately recognized that Prosper and Martine Assouline had founded a publishing house unlike any other when it designed Assouline's New York office. The project was so successful—acknowledging that the publisher of lavish coffee table books on art, architecture, design, fashion, photography, gastronomy, lifestyle and travel was also a savvy curator and marketer of Assouline-branded home furnishings, art, antiques, gifts and accessories—BR Design was hired to design Maison Assouline Dubai for the Fashion Avenue section of The Dubai Mall in Dubai, United Arab Emirates. Like its predecessor, the Maison Assouline London, the luxury concept store for culture was conceptualized as "a refuge for those seeking style, culture and art de vivre." Indeed, the two-story, 7,000-square-foot space has been likened to a cabinet of curiosities for the affluent, a lavishly appointed contemporary bookstore, gift boutique, and furniture, art and antiques gallery where customers can relax at the Swans Bar, a bar and restaurant evoking Hollywood in the 1930s, a landscaped terrace overlooking the Dubai Fountain, or a private room where the staff can assist customers in making special purchases. If Emiratis were to choose the Maison Assouline Dubai as a favored gathering place, who would blame them?

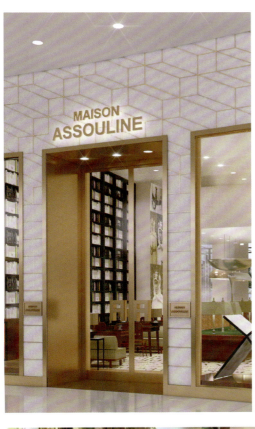

Elizabeth Arden

China

With Chinese consumers returning to retail stores, Elizabeth Arden, a major American cosmetics, skin care and fragrance company, anticipates a healthy rebound in sales. Young women in China have favored the brand for its quality products and its media-savvy and culturally sensitive marketing. Elizabeth Arden pays close attention to Chinese consumer culture, anticipating what young women want by offering continually updated choices. It also makes important alliances with Chinese "key opinion leaders"—social media influencers like hit idol Hu Yitian—who are avidly followed by gen Zers and Millennials. BR Design's competition entry for Elizabeth Arden's new retail prototype for China builds on the rapport between the brand and its customers. In a configuration that can range from 2,000 to 3,000 square feet, the design features a beauty salon, where customers can receive beauty treatments and view product displays, adjacent to an elegant boudoir, where they can sample products and make purchases. Outfitted with a variety of cosmetic display wall cabinets, display counters and shop furniture, the prototype contrasts the cool modernity of the salon with the lush, garden-like boudoir. Might "a spa day at Elizabeth Arden" become a cherished experience in China? The prototype strongly suggests that it could.

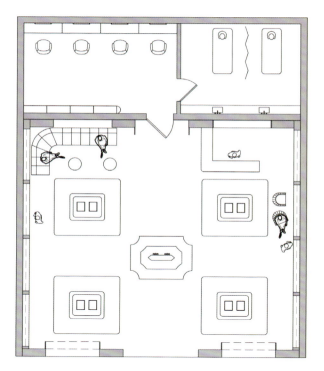

Columbia Properties Rooftop Terrace

New York, New York

The tenants of 1370 Broadway, a 16-story, 279,533-square-foot office building in midtown Manhattan's Times Square South neighborhood, recently discovered an urban oasis directly above their heads: a stylish, contemporary, 3,200-square-foot rooftop lounge designed by BR Design. The project is part of a capital improvement program by the landlord that has brought a new lobby and building entrance, modernized elevator cabs and new freight elevator, and new bathrooms and common corridors to a structure built in 1922. A rooftop lounge has become a prized amenity for office tenants nationwide, in sharp contrast to the traditional view of rooftop real estate as a no-man's land for chimneys, water tanks, antennas and HVAC equipment. To make the lounge a reality, BR Design reconfigured the roof, relocating rooftop air conditioning units and designing an open space featuring a variety of seating areas, a serving counter for food and drink, and a dramatic promenade overlooking midtown Manhattan. Using attractive but durable materials, including metal, wood, paving stones, outdoor furniture and architectural lighting fixtures—while skillfully concealing a skylight by enclosing it within a planter bordered by banquette seating—BR Design has given 1370 Broadway tenants an inspired way to escape the office without leaving it.

Carvart

New York, New York

Mention Carvart to leading architects and interior designers and you conjure countless aesthetic and functional possibilities for environments exploiting the unique properties of glass. The manufacturer of architectural glass products and hardware systems has worked with top architecture and interior design firms, glaziers, contractors and various industry partners for over 20 years, combining precision engineering, innovative industrial design and expert service to produce outstanding installations in all 50 states and worldwide. To develop Carvart's new, one-floor, 15,000-square-foot studio headquarters in the heart of Times Square, New York's legendary theater district, BR Design designed the showroom and office as a single, unified environment, giving staff members and visitors a continuous demonstration of the company's capabilities by incorporating a generous assortment of its products in the contemporary interior. The design employed modern furnishings and a neutral color palette to allow the various glass components to display their utility and aesthetics, and the results were dazzling. Beginning with a reception area dominated by a long, multi-purpose reception desk that could also be used for cooking, dining, presentations and meetings, the interiors included open plan workstations, private offices and conference rooms, all exploiting the functional versatility and sheer beauty of architectural glass by Carvart.

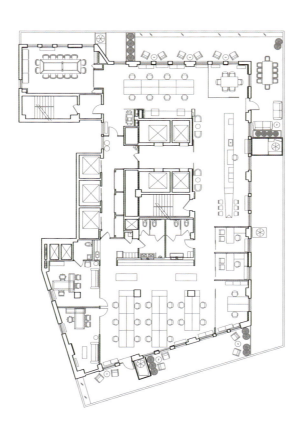

High Line Residence

New York, New York

New York's High Line is a 1.45-mile-long linear park built on an abandoned New York Central Railroad elevated spur running along Manhattan's West Side from the Meatpacking District north to the West Side Yard. It is a unique and mesmerizing public amenity born of urban archaeology and landscape architecture and has made its presence unmistakably known. While millions of visitors stroll among its meticulously cultivated plantings, the historic commercial neighborhood is witnessing a massive surge in real estate development. The 2,730-square-foot High Line Residence designed by BR Design Associates gives the client an appropriate contemporary space in this rapidly transforming community. It is ideal to entertain and showcase a modern art collection by providing a gallery, living/dining room, kitchen, master bedroom suite, guest bedroom and bathroom, den and balcony. The space is designed to be savored from afar and close up. Within a finely crafted architectural interior of wood, leather, metal and stone are open spaces with generous outdoor views framed by fine contemporary furnishings, including many bespoke pieces designed by BR Design and the Uhuru workshop. There is specialized lighting for the art collection and architectural details such as a handsome metal feature wall--a tantalizing vision of 21st-century urban living.

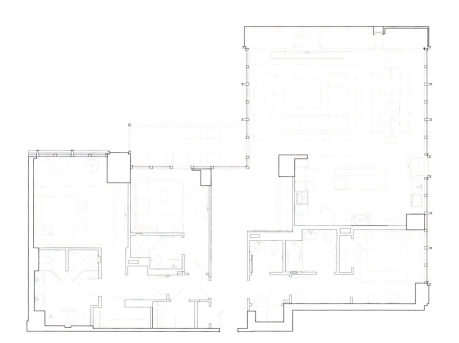

Conde Nast F.I.G

Brooklyn, New York

Launched in 2014 to generate imaginative food content for a diverse and appreciative audience of 86 million consumers from award-winning traditional and digital media brands--Bon Appétit, Epicurious.com, The Farm, FIG Influencers Network, Healthy-ish, Basic and City Guides--the Food Innovation Group (F.I.G.) of Condé Nast has also been a success to major food industry advertisers looking for impact through advertising network buys. To give F.I.G. personnel state-of-the-art offices, test and shoot kitchens, BR Design inserted state-of-the-art engineering systems, contemporary office space and three shoot kitchens, each configured with its own aesthetics to support a different editorial theme, within the shell of a structure in Brooklyn's Industry City, a 35-acre complex of industrial buildings dating from 1907, without concealing the raw space's original character. The contrast between modern electrical, mechanical and plumbing systems components and the building's century-old concrete floors, columns and ceilings, steel factory windows and time-worn wood strip flooring gave this media laboratory for food preparation a vibrant and decidedly edgy character that was perfectly suited to F.I.G.'s staff and operations. Like the stream of delicious food content that F.I.G. produced, the F.I.G. workspace offered fresh proof that creative cooking combines new tastes with traditional cuisine and timeless ingredients.

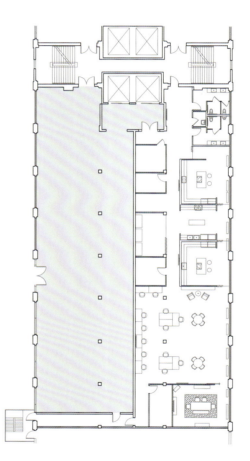

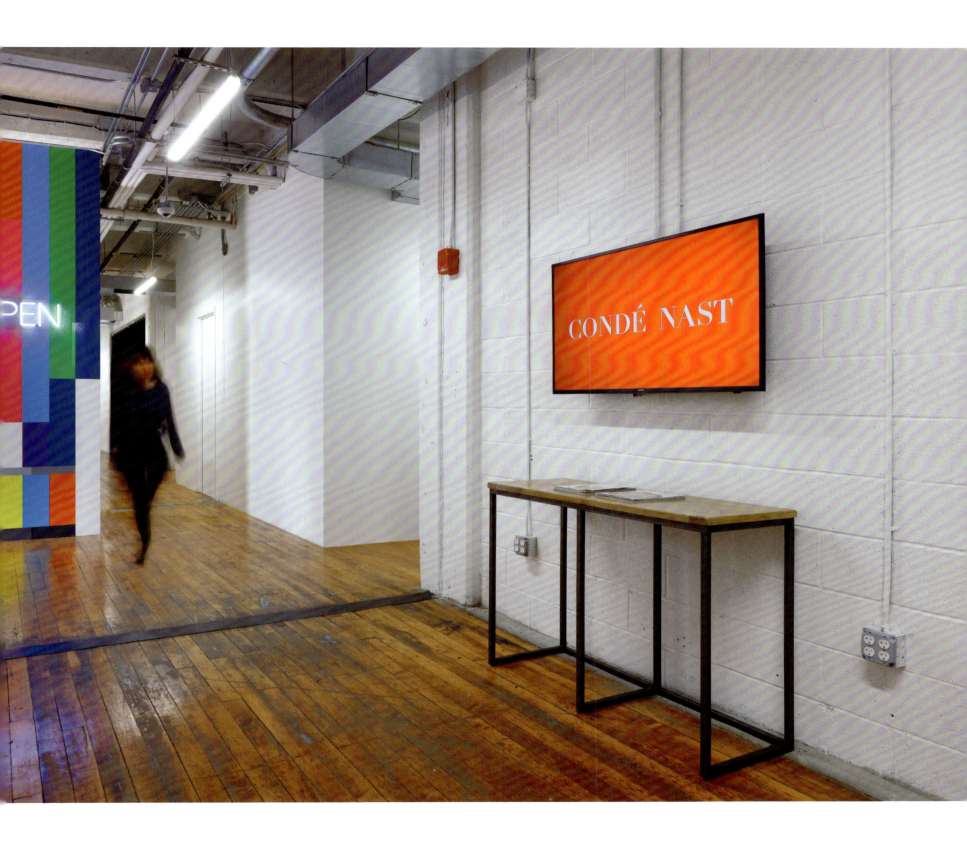

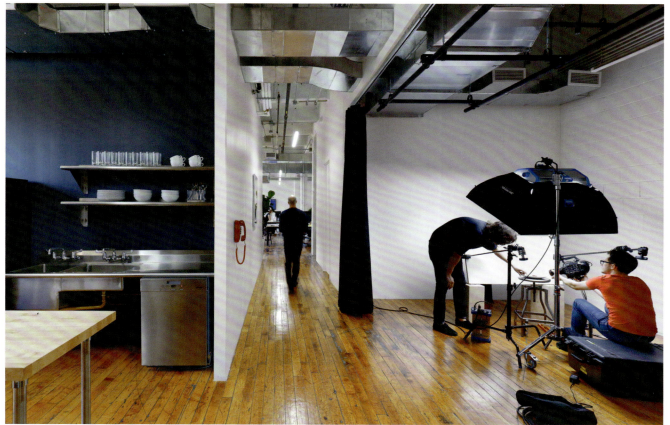

Unite Us

New York, New York

Unite Us is a healthcare technology company that builds coordinated care networks of health and social service providers. By standardizing how health and social care providers communicate and monitor outcomes together, Unite Us can align all stakeholders from healthcare, government and community around a shared goal to improve health. As a result, providers across sectors can send and receive secure referrals, track every patient's total health journey, and report on tangible outcomes across a full range of services in a centralized, cohesive, and collaborative ecosystem. Unite Us's platform is the unifying infrastructure between healthcare entities and community-based organizations, and its network services comprises teams of experts who build your network from the ground up. BR Design recently completed the design of a new, 30,000-square-foot, two-floor headquarters for 200 employees of Unite Us in New York's Financial District. The contemporary workplace, providing glass-fronted conference rooms, open workstations, collaborative areas, phone rooms, reception area, and pantries and other support facilities, is characterized by the complete absence of private offices. All staff members, from the CEO to the intern, occupy the same size workstation, an appropriate arrangement for an organization whose mission is to bring together all stakeholders involved in a community's wellbeing.

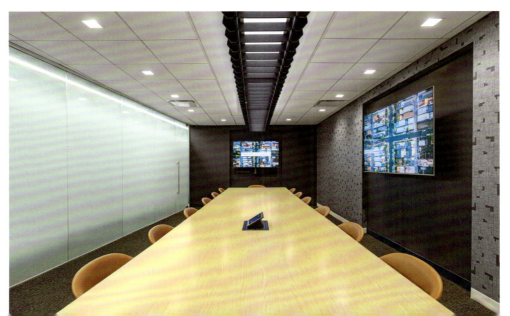

East End Capital

New York, New York

Veterans of the real estate industry can recall a time when pre-built office space—the commercial office market's version of what the fashion world calls prêt-à-porter—was viewed as inferior to custom designed and constructed facilities. These relatively small offices are carved out of larger floors to entice boutique tenants that lack the time, inclination or budget to undertake the traditional build-to-suit design and construction process, but they are not humble abodes any more. At the request of the developer of a Manhattan office building, BR Design provided space planning and interior design for upscale pre-built offices of 4,000 to 7,500 square feet on four floors, comprising perimeter private offices, interior workstations, pantries and reception areas that epitomize the versatile floor plans, quality construction and good design that today's tenants want. In fact, BR Design has incorporated wood and stone millwork, glass office fronts, handsome contemporary furnishings, striking architectural lighting and a warm, neutral color scheme in these projects that can appeal to high-end firms in finance, law and other professions. The spaces offer the allure of state-of-the-art accommodations that are ready to put to work immediately.

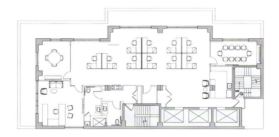

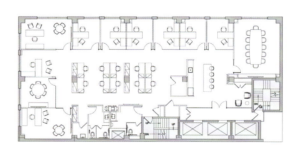

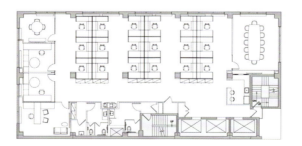

Richard James

New York, New York

Richard James is a contemporary British house of eye-catching bespoke, and ready-to-wear men's clothing. The company was founded on London's Savile Row in 1992 by designer Richard James and business partner Sean Dixon to pursue a straight forward yet daring business strategy: produce classic men's clothing of exceptional quality and push the boundaries through color, cut and design. To give Richard James an appropriate retail setting in New York, BR Design worked with Andy Martin Architects, designer of the company's flagship Savile Row store, to create a one-floor, 3,000-square-foot store within a landmarked building on prestigious Park Avenue. Following the configuration of the Savile Row store, the Park Avenue floor plan was divided into distinct bespoke and ready-to-wear areas by a shimmering, floor-to-ceiling dichroic screen that filters colors and changes luminosity during the day. The screen was key to a total composition that included a luminous ceiling, brushed metal wall panels, custom-designed angular display cases and seating, and minimalist store fixtures, projecting a futurist image to attract fashion-forward shoppers. Richard James proudly noted that this marked the first time a Savile Row House offered its full bespoke, made-to-measure and ready-to-wear services in New York, and it did so with panache.

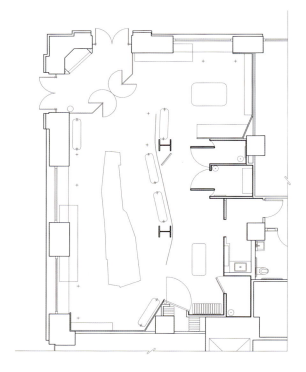

Edward Fields Carpet Makers

New York, New York

Renowned custom carpet maker Edward Fields (1913-1979) liked to declare that there was "no limit to carpet design." Fortunately, luxury carpets and rugs like those Edward Fields Carpet Makers created for Hollywood stars such as Princess Grace of Monaco and Mary Tyler Moore as well as U.S. Presidents Eisenhower, Kennedy, Nixon and Johnson will continue to dazzle architects, designers and their clients. The company's new, one-floor, 5,000-square-foot Manhattan office, design studio and showroom, designed by BR Design, helps ensure this. The facility's opening comes at an important moment for the company, which was purchased in 2005 by Tai Ping Carpets, a Hong Kong-based custom carpet manufacturer. A new branding campaign celebrates the steady commitment to Field's credo of every product being bespoke, tailored to the exact aesthetic vision and practical requirement of the customer. BR Design's solution shrewdly underplays the physical environment, which is characterized by a neutral color scheme, wood millwork, concrete floors, Mid-Century modern furnishings and track lighting. This serves to showcase the carpets and rugs--thousands of samples are stored here--in all their splendor. The new setting prompted a company official to comment, "Due to the new branding and identity of the showroom, sales have increased dramatically."

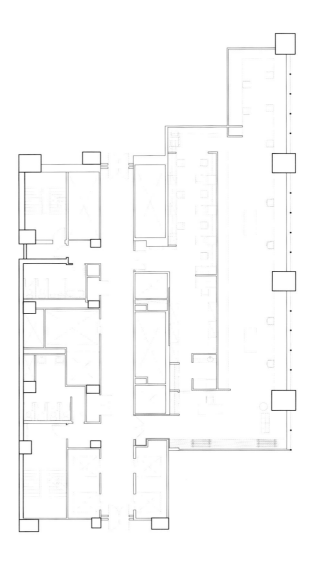

Greenwich Residence

Greenwich, CT

Who could resist the funky, tree house spirit of the three-story (plus loft), 1960s single-family house in Greenwich, Connecticut that a family retained BR Design Associates to update? The family's objectives were straight-forward: modernize the plumbing, open up closed-off areas, create a second-floor master suite, and transform the first floor into an open space for entertaining. Fortunately, the house was sturdily constructed and well maintained, with a two-story entry and living room highlighting a bright, airy interior. BR Design's challenge was to introduce contemporary technology, accommodations and amenities while preserving the wood structure's original character. The completed renovation produced a remodeled kitchen, new guest bath, and new wine room for the first floor. On the second floor: new, cable-strung stair, elevated walkway and mezzanine, and new master suite, comprising bedroom, bathroom and dressing room were created. A new guest bathroom for the third floor, and a new, second-floor dormer and paint for the exterior completed the project. The resulting space was fresh and timeless, artfully blending new construction in wood, stone, tile and glass, new furnishings and a sparkling array of new, custom lighting fixtures. The existing interiors and the family's collections of modern art and Mid-Century furnishings completed a warm, stylish, year-round tree house for the young at heart.

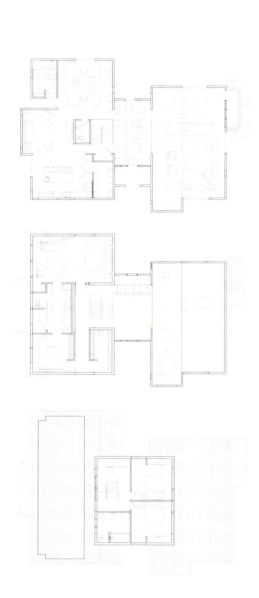

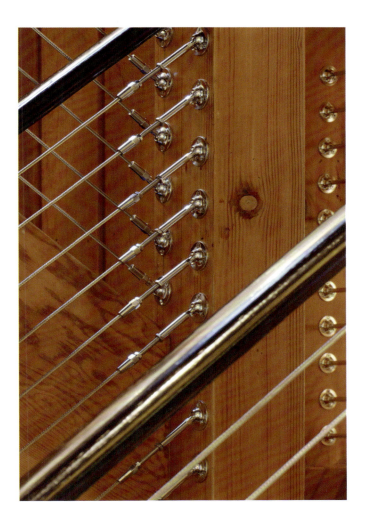

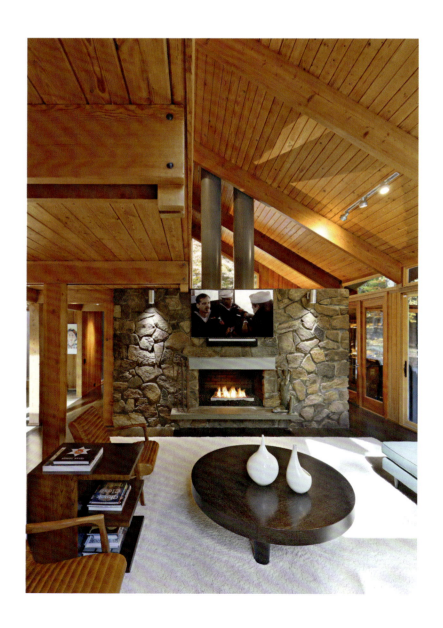

Harry's of London

New York, New York

Creating stylish, high-end contemporary British footwear engineered for comfort--thanks to its signature Technogel innersole--has been the mission of Harry's of London since 2001. The company began with sleek, sporty styles that attracted immediate notice and became the benchmark for all that followed at such prestigious retailers as Bloomingdale's, Neiman Marcus and Nordstrom. For its first New York retail store, Harry's of London retained BR Design to work with New York-based French designer Christian Lahoude to design a space on the ground floor of a landmark building on Park Avenue. The opulent store front was designed with restraint, in keeping with the building's status as a landmark. However, the interior was modeled to explicitly complement the sleek shoes from Harry's of London with a luxurious setting featuring Italian gray marble, an oak herringbone floor, engraved paneled mirrors, and custom shelving, lighting and furniture. If the result was unapologetically elitist, it was also in keeping with the objectives of the company's CEO Steven Newey, who told Forbes in 2017, "My vision, our mission for the brand, is for it to become the go-to brand for men's shoes globally."

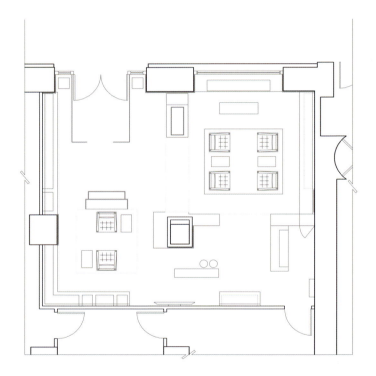

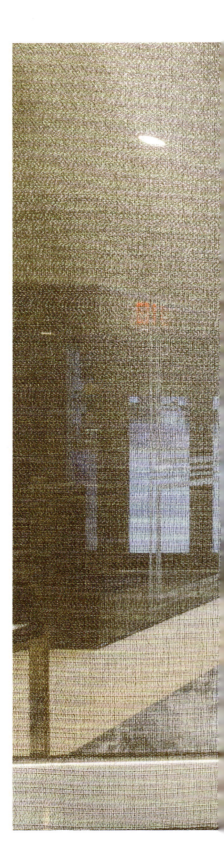

Winklevoss Capital

New York, New York

Where start-up enterprises begin their precarious infancy is no mystery to the venture capitalists financing them to find "the next big thing." So when Winklevoss Capital Management, founded by Tyler and Cameron Winklevoss, retain BR Design to help create a one-floor, 5,000-square-foot office for 30-plus people in New York's Flatiron District, they decisively addressed the issue. As Tyler Winklevoss told The New York Times, "We recognize in New York there's difficulty in bridging that gap between working in Starbucks or your living room and actually having the money to get your own space." The new, contemporary facility, comprising an open office with bench-style workstations, large conference room, small conference ("huddle") rooms, pantry/meeting area and DJ booth/bar as well as private offices for the Winklevosses, functions as an "incubator." Here, start-ups in the company portfolio can grow before investing in their own offices. Featuring exposed ceilings and building systems, open workstations, glass partitions, industrial lighting, carpet tile and wood floors the high-tech space deliberately resists being all work and no play. Playful touches include a refined, white-and-gray color palette spiked with pink, an array of classic modern furnishings, iPad-driven environmental controls, and the DJ booth/bar, which brings after-hours events to life for staff and visitors.

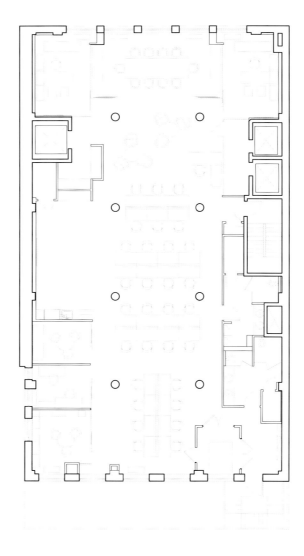

Martha Stewart Living Omnimedia

New York, New York

The one-story, 150,000-square-foot New York office for some 500 employees of Martha Stewart Living Omnimedia doesn't resemble the domestic settings that appear in the media company's books, magazines, catalogues, television programs and product packaging. However, it has been planned, designed and constructed with the same meticulous care. BR Design, serving in the role of associate architect to the firm of Daniel Rowen Architect, has provided space planning, design development, construction documents and project management for this ambitious facility. Located within the Starrett Lehigh Building, an Art Deco-style industrial landmark structure, the award-winning space uses an "open architecture" approach to planning that preserves much of the powerful, original interior architecture. Yet the design provides maximum flexibility and deep penetration of natural light and views to such facilities as photography studios, test kitchens, prop library, woodworking shop, merchandising center, computer facilities, and open plan and private offices. The offices themselves are specially configured to maintain the overall feeling of openness. For example, a custom made workstation for open areas has been created from an industrial "kit of parts" to encourage communication and collaboration. As for private office spaces, they are located along the interior with full-height glass fronts to take advantage of the inward transfer of natural light. Quite impressive for a behind the scenes workspace that the company's customers will never see.

Square Mile Capital

New York, New York

Square Mile Capital Management is recognized as a leading investment manager serving institutional and private investors by successfully investing in commercial real estate at all points in the market cycle. They commissioned BR Design Associates to renovate its one-floor, 10,000-square-foot office in midtown Manhattan. Square Mile requested a new professional environment that would be simultaneously modern and timeless. To satisfy the company, the design team created a contemporary workplace for the reception area, private offices, open office areas (featuring custom open desking workstations designed by BR Design), conference rooms, lounge, pantry, restrooms and elevator lobby. The design incorporates such timeless materials as wood, stone, carpet and glass. It also includes such modern flourishes as wood wall paneling accents that are characterized by slender, horizontal bands alternating with deep reveals, and floor-to-ceiling glass walls and doors for all enclosed spaces to enhance the sense of openness and to infuse corridors and interior spaces with daylight and views. Handsome classic mid-century modern furnishings, cool, minimal architectural lighting fixtures, and an eclectic sampling of contemporary art make the space effective and comfortable. Thus the 30 employees of Square Mile are able to focus their attention on real estate investments opportunities in major markets across the nation.

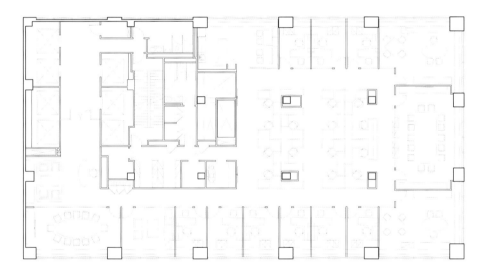

Joele Frank, Wilkinson Brimmer & Katcher

New York, New York

Leading professional firms in such fields as law, accounting, advertising, public relations, investment banking and design know their clients well, and their workplaces show it. For Joele Frank, Wilkinson Brimmer Katcher, an award-winning public relations firm specializing in strategic financial communications and investor relations, the commission it awarded to BR Design Associates was for its one-floor, 27,000-square-foot New York office. It functions as a dignified, serene and well-tailored corporate setting where boards of directors could deal with activist investors or senior executives could map out M&A strategy. That is exactly what awaits employees and clients, in what could easily be a Fortune 500 company's headquarters, BR Design has conceived a contemporary environment. The space comprises a reception area resembling a university club lounge, handsome perimeter offices and conference rooms enclosed in floor-to-ceiling glass, simple open workstations discreetly bordered by frosted-glass-topped partitions, and an informal pantry suited to lively give and take conversations, all encircled by stunning views of the New York skyline. As could be expected, every design detail has received close attention. The careful zoning of activities, the selection of quality materials and classic modern furnishings ensure the facility can perform as flawlessly as the firm itself.

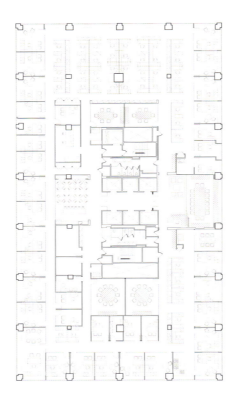

Schwartz & Benjamin

New York, New York

Schwartz & Benjamin is a family-owned foot-wear licensing company founded in 1923. Working with such leading brand-name fashion houses as Kate Spade, Rebecca Minkoff, Alice+Olivia, and Derek Lam, Schwartz & Benjamin serves retailers, distributors and consumers in North America, Europe and Asia. The company's recently completed, three-floor, 15,000-square foot New York office, housing 40 employees in sales showrooms and a product development studio, was designed by BR Design Associates to support its roles as a designer, manufacturer, importer and distributor. Schwartz & Benjamin represents multiple businesses with strong brand identities. The project's chief design problem was to create a unified, cohesive gallery-like space where the different partners occupy separate galleries within the architectural envelope. The space includes showrooms, open offices, private and semi-private offices, conference rooms, open storage, print/copy areas, reception, lounges, pantries and elevator lobbies. The 9th floor houses the production team; on the 10th floor showrooms share space with reception, customer pantry and offices for brand management, and the 11th floor pairs showrooms with offices for executives and sales team members. Together they show how effectively color, lighting and furnishings can differentiate the perception of space.

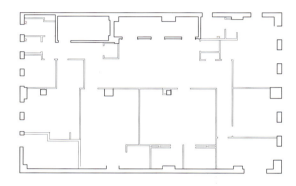

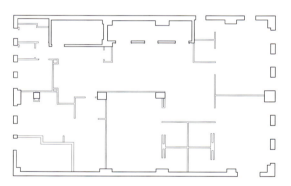

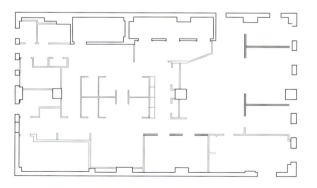

Hoboken Residence

Hoboken, New Jersey

The greening of Hoboken, New Jersey, that began in the late 1970s continues with subtle additions like the four-story, 5,000-square-foot townhouse recently designed for a young family by BR Design, placing a completely new structure behind an existing, historic façade. Retaining the existing basement, which was enlarged, the project replaced the existing space with new first, second and third floors. The new residence was conceived to immerse the family in a stylish, contemporary environment for gracious living and entertaining, with large expanses of glass on the new, rear-facing façade bringing abundant daylight and exterior views indoors. Accommodations included a first floor featuring a sunken living room with 13-foot-high ceiling and 13-foot-high sliding glass doors without a transom, a dining room with built-in storage, butler's pantry, powder room and eat-in kitchen, a second floor organized as a children's floor with two bedrooms, bathroom and laundry room, and a third floor housing a master bedroom suite, exercise room, office and guest bedroom and bath. Even the roof and basement were designed for active use. A kitchen, island/bar and seating area made the roof an attractive fair weather amenity, while a family room, bar, and full bathroom welcomed eveyone to the basement year-round.

Jewelry Showroom

New York, New York

Now in its 80th year of business and third generation of family ownership, this Jewelry company is a leading New York based diamond merchant offering certified diamonds of the highest quality and sourcing. To enhance the customer experience and display its products in a museum-quality environment, the company retained BR Design to design an exclusive, appointment-only office and showroom on Fifth Avenue in Manhattan's celebrated Diamond District. The contemporary design drew on strong, horizontal forms, refined construction detailing, high-quality natural materials, and superior craftsmanship to produce a space that is spare, elegant and inviting. Walnut was used for millwork and flooring, for example, while wool carpet was placed in selected showroom and office areas, and clear and frosted glass panels were positioned to allow daylight and views of Midtown Manhattan to flow throughout the space. Sophisticated lighting was carefully aimed to draw attention to product displays at the same time it bathed the overall space in a luxurious glow. As a finishing touch, the showroom was furnished with classic Modern pieces from such masters as Mies van der Rohe, Charles Eames and Warren Platner.

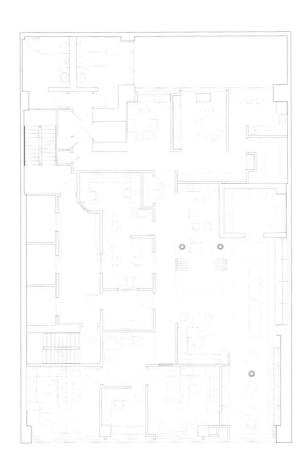

251 West 39th Street

New York, New York

Ion Media Networks

New York, New York

What kind of workplace befits a U.S. television broadcaster with 60-plus stations reaching 260 million viewers? A visit to the New York office of Ion Media Networks, a two-floor, 30,000-square-foot space designed by BR Design Associates, reveals that it is open, versatile and memorable. BR Design, designer of Ion's previous New York facility, was retained to create an open environment for employee interaction and corporate branding. The new office, typified by low-paneled workstations and glass-enclosed private spaces, displays captivating focal points and original details. Along with such basic accommodations as the reception area, open and private offices, and conference rooms are such destinations as the staircase, breakout area and main conference room. The staircase, framed by a glass-and-stainless-steel guardrail, is crowned by a glowing soffit with a spectacular custom lighting fixture of metal mesh drapery, ideal for social encounters. The breakout area, adjacent to the staircase, is enclosed by a graceful, curving folding/stacking wall system, an outstanding way to accommodate special events. The main conference room can "disappear" at will thanks to switchable glass technology providing privacy when needed. Even the color scheme makes a statement, mixing a predominately white palette with white maple and Ion's corporate blue to paint an ethereally beautiful landscape.

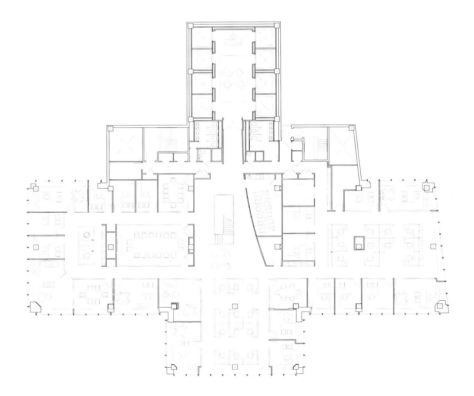

McCann Erickson

Detroit, Michigan

Sometimes the best way to get a fresh perspective on life is to move. That's one of the benefits of McCann Erickson Detroit's relocation from Troy, Michigan's second largest city, with 80,980 residents (2010 Census) and the headquarters of numerous automotive and financial companies, to Birmingham, an affluent Detroit suburb with a population of 20,103 (2010 Census) where wealthy Detroit families have lived since its incorporation in 1864. The 350-person advertising agency is part of McCann-Erickson Worldwide, a global advertising agency with offices in 130-plus countries. They serve such major clients as General Motors and Chevrolet from a three-story, 90,000-square-foot office, designed by BR Design Associates, in a former department store. In its private offices, open-plan workstations, conference rooms, reception area, café and support facilities, McCann Erickson enjoys a lively, open, interactive environment. A central vertical circulation well, incorporating existing escalators and a new, bleacher-style stairway that doubles as a meeting area, also encourages collaboration. Appointed in terrazzo flooring, glass walls, and classic modern furnishings, the one-time store now sells ideas as its merchandise. This allows the venerable advertising agency, founded in 1902, to work more effectively with GM, its top Motor City client, founded just six years after McCann Erickson.

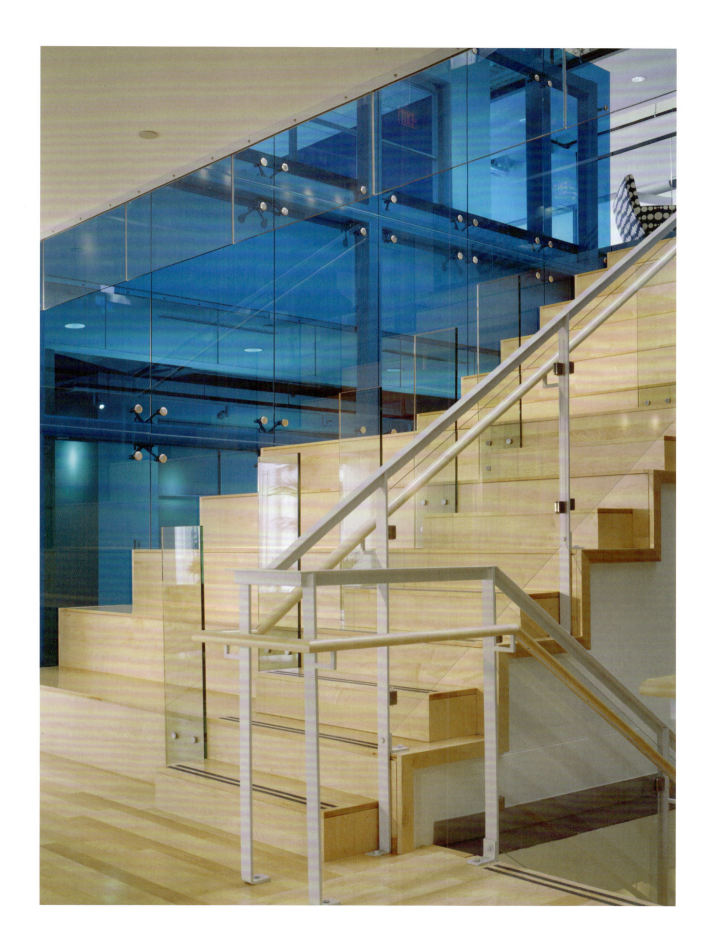

BR Design Associates

New York, New York

Trust an accomplished, award-winning interior design firm to know when and why its workplace no longer works and what to do about it. BR Design Associates recognized that it was time for a new home when its fragmented existing space seriously impeded the teamwork and internal communication that drive its activities. The new, 5,000-square-foot studio, located in the landmark Film Center Building, clearly promotes collaboration. Its studio places most employees in open office benching, with the private executive office employing a glass wall and door to preserve the open feeling. The composition incorporates polished concrete floors and exposed slabs to add character to cool white walls, ceilings, furniture and finishes, black window treatments, carpet tile and pin-up boards, and white marble counters in the pantry and the library. The overall environment feels clean, crisp and invigorating. An artistic gesture does appear in the curving wall with a backlit BR Design logo that greets visitors. Yet it is also a cost-effective gesture that generates a natural flow into the office, one of many reassuring signs that good design supports a client's culture rather than a designer's ego.

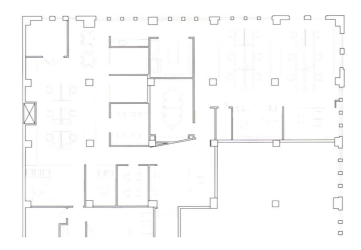

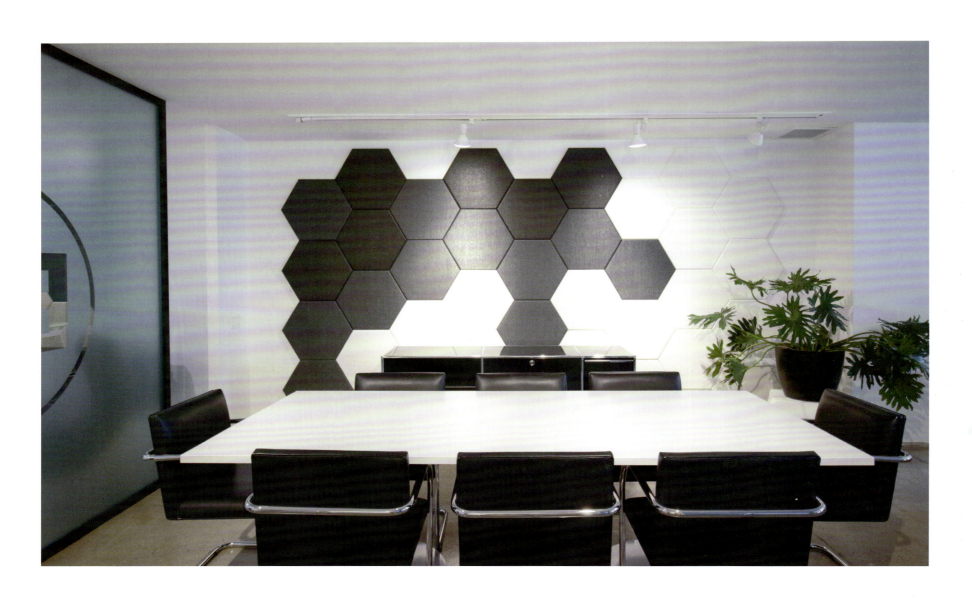

Ignition One
New York, NY
20,000 RSF
2017

1440 Broadway
New York, NY
35,000 RSF
2016

Digital Evolution
New York, NY
12,700 RSF
2015

Caché
New York, NY
75,000 RSF
2015

SumAll
New York, NY
12,700 RSF
2015

Deer Stags
New York, NY
15,000 RSF
2012

Cake & Arrow
New York, NY
15,000 RSF
2011

Tai Ping Carpets
New York, NY
12,500 RSF
2006

Benhar
New York, NY
7,500 RSF
2006

Gruntal & Co.
New York, NY
300,000 RSF
2005

Somerset Partners
New York, NY
5,000 RSF
2005

Data Broadcasting
New York, NY
30,000 RSF
2000

BR Design
New York, NY
10,000 RSF
2000

Draft Worldwide
New York, NY
60,000 SF
1995

Merill Lynch
Chicago, IL
100,000 RSF
1995

Barns & Noble.com
New York, NY
100,000 RSF
1999

Sullivan & Liapakis
New York, NY
55,000 RSF
1993

CREDITS

Amit Children
Photographer: Eric Laignel

Assouline
Photographer: Tom Sibley
GC: Cohen Brothers
MEP: Jack Green Associates

BR Design
Photographer: Tatiana Rampersaud & Tom Sibley
GC: Stepping Stone Construction Management

Committee to Protect Journalists
Photographer: Eric Laignel

Cooper Robertson
Photographer: Tom Sibley
GC: Stepping Stone Construction Management
MEP: CFS Engineering

Greenwich Residence
Photographer: Tom Sibley
GC: Justino Contracting
Millwork: Bilotta Kitchen

Edward Fields
Photographer: Eric Laignel
GC: Lehr Construction
MEP: Consentini Associates

Elite Daily
Photographer: Tom Sibley
GC: Stepping Stone Construction Management
MEP: Jack Green Associates

Galvanize
Photographer: Eric Laignel
GC: Stepping Stone Construction Management
MEP: MG Engineering

Highline Residence
Photographer: Tom Sibley

Ignition One
Photographer: Tom Sibley
GC: JRM
MEP: MG Engineering

Ion Media Networks
Photographer: Tom Sibley
GC: J.T. Magen & Company Inc.
MEP: Cosentini Associates

Joele Frank
Photographer: Tom Sibley
GC: Cohen Brothers
MEP: Cosentini Associates

Marx Realty
Photographer: Tatiana Rampersaud

McCann Erickson
GC: Turner Construction

Neoscape
Photographer: Tom Sibley
GC: Stepping Stone Construction Management
MEP: Jack Green Associates

Martha Stewart Living Omnimedia
GC: Americon Construction
MEP: Ambrosino, DePinto & Schmieder Consulting Engineers

Schwartz & Benjamin
Photographer: Rebecca McAlpin
GC: Icon Interiors
MEP: MG Engineering

Schwartz & Benjamin
Photographer: Mark Ross
GC: MBI Group
MEP: Cosentini Associates

Square Mile Capital
Photographer: Tom Sibley
GC: Icon Interiors
MEP: Cosentini Associates

Tai Ping
Photographer: Eric Laignel
GC: Alcon Construction
MEP: Ambrosino, DePinto & Schmieder Consulting Engineers

The Rohaytn Group
Photographer: Eric Laignel
GC: Icon Interiors

Winklevoss Capital
Photographer: Tom Sibley
GC: JT Magen & Company Inc.

545 Madison, 2nd Floor
Photographer: Tatiana Rampersaud

Floorplans: Son Nguyen Viet

ACKNOWLEDGEMENTS

The public likes to think of the interior designer as a singular genius, working alone in a studio, lavishing attention on every detail of a project. It's an appealing fantasy. But consider what goes into a contemporary commercial interior space.

Today's modern office, for example, is a complex environment designed to perform multiple functions for the client organization, accommodate a diverse population of occupants, support a multitude of technological systems, provide safety, security and optimum environmental conditions, and yes, project a visual image consistent with the identity and goals of the client. Yes, interior designers like to think of their work as art. Aesthetics are just one part of the total package, however.

For this reason, BR Design wishes to thank the individuals and firms that have contributed to the success of its projects. In addition to our staff members past and present, we salute the architects and engineers who aid and coordinate our designs, the vendors of construction materials, building systems and interior furnishings who interpret our designs, the contractors, technicians and craftsmen who build our designs, and the professionals in real estate, law, finance and government who shepherd our designs from concept to reality.

Of course, we could not do any of the above without our clients. You have turned our visions for a better world into everyday reality for countless people over the last 35 years. To you we express our deepest thanks.